OXFORD
UNIVERSITY PRESS

Anna had come to stay for a few days. Kipper and Anna did a drawing, then Kipper read his book with Mum.

"That's very good, Kipper," said
Mum. "Now, I'm going to make an
extra big pizza."

"Get me the tomato puree out of
the cupboard, please," said Mum.
"Here it is," said Kipper.

The pizza was ready, so they all
took a slice.

"This tastes like strawberry and
tomato," said Chip. "Strawmato!"

"Yuk, you used strawberry sauce
instead of tomato puree," said Biff.

"They do look alike," said Mum.

"Didn't you notice either, Kipper?"

"The label looked a bit fuzzy,"
said Kipper. "It's like at school when
I look at the board. And my head
aches sometimes too."

"Then we'd both better have our
eyes tested," said Mum.

"We might get glasses like Anna,"
said Kipper.

So the next day Mum, Kipper and
Anna went to the optician.

"I'm Alison," said Ms Lask. "I'm
just going to check your eyes."

"I'm going to make everything
blurry, then I'll shine a light into
your eyes," said Alison. "Keep
looking at the light in the mirror."

"Show me the letter that you can see in the mirror," said Alison.

Kipper pointed to the letter on the card.

"What can you see through these funny glasses?" said Alison.

"Which lens is better, one or two?"

"Which circles look darker, the red or the green?"

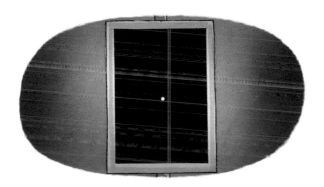

"Which side of the light is the line? Or is it in the middle?"

"You're doing very well, Kipper,"
said the optician. "Now, I'm going to
move this stick closer and closer. Tell
me when you see two clowns."

Alison gave Kipper a book. "Look
at this page," she said.

"Ah," said the optician. "I know
why the board at school looks fuzzy."

"Your eyes are fine, Kipper. You just need to hold the book further away when you're reading," said Alison, "and sit up straight.

If you hold the book too close,
your eyes get used to it. Then things
further away look fuzzy. Like the
board at school."

Kipper told everyone about the
eye test. "It was fun," he said. "I just
have to hold my book further away
when I'm reading."

Dad read them a book about eyes.

"I wish I could see in the dark like owls and cats," said Kipper.

"Then eat your carrots!" said Dad.

"How about carrot cake?" said
Kipper.

"Good idea," said Dad. "I'll make
one. I've got a new recipe to try."

Dad's carrot cake was ready to bake. "Gas mark 8 and it will be ready in 2 hours," he said to himself.

Later, Dad had to sew on a button,
but he couldn't thread the needle.
"Here, you do it, Biff," he said.
"You've got sharp eyes."

"What's all that smoke?" said Anna.
Everyone ran into the kitchen.
Smoke was coming out of the oven.
Oh no! Dad's cake was burned.

"It says gas mark 3 not 8," said
Biff. "It's cinder cake not carrot
cake. Oh Dad, you need to get your
eyes tested, too!"

Talk about the story

How did the strawberry sauce get onto the pizza?

Why did Mum and Kipper go to the optician?

What did the optician tell Kipper to do?

If things looked fuzzy to you, who would you tell?

How to look after your eyes

Do

Sit up nice and straight
when you're reading,
writing or drawing.

Wear sunglasses when
you are in strong sunshine.

Have your eyes
tested regularly.

Tell a grown up if you get
headaches or things look fuzzy.

Don't

Don't hold your book too close when you're reading.

Don't put your nose on the desk when you're writing or drawing.

Don't look directly at the sun.

Don't shine lights in anyone's eyes.

Why is it important to look after your eyes?

Which glasses?

Match the right glasses to the six people.